Animal Neighbours
Duck

Stephen Savage

HODDER
Wayland

An imprint of Hodder Children's Books

Animal Neighbours

Titles in this series:

**Badger • Bat • Blackbird • Deer • Duck • Fox
Hare • Hedgehog • Mole • Mouse • Otter • Owl
Rat • Snake • Swallow • Toad**

**For more information on this series and other Hodder Wayland titles,
go to www.hodderwayland.co.uk**

Conceived and produced for Hodder Wayland by

Nutshell
MEDIA

Intergen House, 65–67 Western Road, Hove BN3 2JQ, UK
www.nutshellmedialtd.co.uk

Commissioning Editor: Vicky Brooker
Designer: Tim Mayer
Illustrator: Jackie Harland
Picture Research: Glass Onion Pictures

Published in Great Britain in 2005 by Hodder Wayland, an imprint of Hodder Children's Books.

British Library Cataloguing in Publication Data
Savage, Stephen, 1965-
Duck. – (Animal neighbours)
1. Ducks – Juvenile literature
I. Title
598.4′1

ISBN 0 7502 4660 X

Cover: A mallard drake on a pond.
Title page: A female mallard's head and beak.

Picture acknowledgements
FLPA 8 (Maurice Walker), 9 (D. Maslowski), 10 (David Hosking), 25 (John Watkins), 28 top (D. Maslowski), 28 right (David Hosking); naturepl.com *Cover* (Niall Benvie), 15 (Dan Burton), 16–17 (Tom Vezo), 19 (Doug Wechsler), 23 (Tom Vezo), 26 (Jean Roche), 28 left (Tom Vezo); NHPA *Title page* (Laurie Campbell), 6 (Manfred Danegger), 7 (Alan Williams), 11 (Ann & Steve Toon), 12 (Roger Tidman), 14 (Guy Edwardes), 17 (Bill Coster), 20 (Laurie Campbell), 21 (Alan Barnes), 22 (Ann & Steve Toon), 24 (Manfred Danegger), 28 bottom (Roger Tidman); OSF 13 (Stan Osolinski), 27 (Richard Packwood).

Printed and bound in China.

Hodder Children's Books
A division of Hodder Headline Limited
338 Euston Road, London NW1 3BH

Contents

Meet the Duck

Ducks are aquatic birds. There are many different species of ducks alive today, living on lakes, ponds and other wetlands throughout the world.

This book looks at the mallard duck, the world's most common species. It can be found across Europe, Asia and North America, and in south-east Australia and New Zealand.

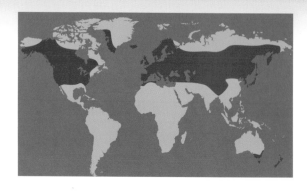

▲ This map shows where the mallard duck lives in the world today.

Wings

The wings are covered in long flight feathers. These are stiffer than the body feathers. They help the duck to fly by pushing against the air.

Tail

Mallards have a short tail. The male has curled central tail feathers, which it uses to attract females.

DUCK FACTS

The mallard duck's scientific name is *Anas platyrhynchos*, which comes from the Latin words *anas* meaning 'duck' and *platyrhynchos* meaning 'broad-billed'.

Male mallards are called drakes and females are called hens. The young are called ducklings. A group of ducks is called a flock.

The mallard's body is about 50–65 cm long. Males weigh an average of 1.2 kg and females weigh about 1 kg.

◄ This shows the size of a mallard duck compared to a domestic cat.

Ears

Ducks do not have external ear flaps. Instead, a small hole leads to an inner ear, which is used to hear predators and the calls of other ducks.

Eyes

Mallards have eyes on the sides of their heads, which helps them spot predators, even from behind.

Nostrils

The nostrils are high up on the beak so the duck can breathe while feeding on the surface of the water.

Beak

The wide, flat beak is a good shape for catching insects on or under the water, and for pulling up weeds and grasses.

Feathers

A downy layer of feathers is covered by a thick, waterproof layer. Trapped air between the layers keeps the duck warm and buoyant. The male has colourful feathers in the breeding season. The rest of the time he is brown like the female.

Body

The round, boat-shaped body and flattened belly help to keep the duck buoyant.

Feet

The feet have three webbed toes pointing forwards and a small hind toe. The webbed toes act as paddles when swimming and help the duck to walk on soft, muddy riverbanks.

▲ **A mallard drake.**

The Duck Family

Ducks belong to the waterfowl family, which also includes geese and swans. There are 147 species of waterfowl, all of which are perfectly adapted to living on or near water. They are excellent swimmers, with strong legs, webbed feet and waterproof feathers. Swans and geese spend much of their time on land, while many ducks live on water for most of the year.

Swans are the largest waterfowl, and getting airborne can sometimes be a problem for such big birds. To be able to fly, swans have to run along the surface of ponds or lakes, beating their wings until they take off.

▼ With a wingspan of around 2 metres, the mute swan is one of the jumbo jets of the bird world. It was given its name because it makes almost no sound except hissing and a few grunts.

▲ A male mandarin duck displays his brightly coloured feathers to a female.

DOMESTIC DUCKS

Mallard ducks were first domesticated over 2,000 years ago, and they are still common on farms today. They have been bred into many different forms that are either tasty to eat or are good egg layers. Over the last 100 years, however, chicken has become more popular than duck meat. Chicken's eggs have also become more popular than duck eggs because they have a milder flavour and a longer shelf life.

Geese are best known for their long migrations from summer breeding grounds to winter feeding grounds. The Greenland white-fronted goose flies 3,200 kilometres non-stop from Greenland to Ireland and Scotland in only 48 hours. Many other geese stop during their journey to feed and rest.

Ducks are one of the smallest types of waterfowl, but they are often the most colourful. One of the most colourful ducks is the male mandarin duck from eastern Asia, which has elaborate feathers to attract females.

Birth and Growing Up

It is early spring, and a female mallard builds a nest, ready to lay her eggs. She makes a cup-shaped nest on the ground from grasses and aquatic plants, and lines it with feathers plucked from her chest. The nest is hidden amongst the tall vegetation surrounding a river or pond, away from the prying eyes of predators.

Very soon the female starts to lay her eggs, one every other day. When the last egg has been laid, she sits on the eggs to keep them warm and safe while the chicks grow inside. By waiting until the last egg has been laid, the duck makes sure all the chicks will hatch at the same time.

▼ As this female mallard sits on her eggs in the nest, her brown feathers help to hide her from predators.

These duck eggs ▶ are just starting to hatch. The ducklings will all emerge at about the same time, which makes it easier for the mother to care for them.

EGGS AND CHICKS

Mallard eggs are a grey-green or sometimes a yellowish-brown colour.

A group of eggs is called a clutch. A group of chicks from the same hatching is called a brood.

There can be between eight and twelve eggs in a clutch, although the average size is ten.

Newly hatched ducklings are also known as 'downies' because of their downy feathers.

The female incubates her eggs in this way for about four weeks, until they are ready to hatch. Once or twice a day she leaves the nest to feed and preen. Before she leaves, she covers the eggs with feathers to keep them warm. Every three to five days, the female turns the eggs using her beak to prevent the embryo from sticking to the inside of the shell.

After four weeks, the ducklings begin to peck their way through the eggshell using the egg tooth on their beak. One after another, the ducklings push the shell apart with their feet until they can poke their head out. A few more pushes and the ducklings are free of their shells.

◀ These ducklings have just hatched from their eggs.

Early days

Wet and exhausted, with their eyes still closed, the ducklings huddle together on the bottom of the nest. Their feathers are yellowy brown, which camouflages them against their surroundings. Within two hours, the ducklings' eyes are open, their feathers are dry and fluffy, and they are able to stand and even walk. The egg tooth drops off soon after hatching since it is no longer needed.

RECOGNISING MOTHER

Just before the ducklings hatch, they call to their mother from inside the egg and their mother calls back. By the time they have hatched, the ducklings know the sound of their mother's quack, which helps keep the family together when they leave the nest. The ducklings also recognise their mother by sight. However, if the first thing they see after hatching is something other than their mother, such as a person, dog, or chicken, the ducklings can mistake it for their mother and follow it instead.

When they are just a few hours old, some of the ducklings will leave the nest and start to peck at their surroundings. They are hungry, but they do not know what is good to eat. Unlike some other birds, ducks do not feed their young. Instead, they lead them to places where they can find food.

The ducklings follow their mother in a single file. She keeps watch to make sure that none get left behind and will quack if she wants them to hurry up. Straggling ducklings can get lost and are easy targets for predators. When their mother stops at a suitable feeding place, the ducklings peck at everything and soon discover what is food.

▼ A mother duck keeps a close eye on her ducklings as she leads them away from the nest for the first time.

Learning to swim and fly

When they are only a day or two old, the female takes her ducklings to the water. Their feathers have been waterproofed with oil from their mother's body. When she enters the water, the ducklings follow. She calls out to any reluctant ducklings, encouraging them into the water.

This is a dangerous time for ducklings. Although they can swim, they cannot yet fly away from predators so it is safer on water than on land.

▼ A female duck leads her large family of thirteen ducklings along the edge of a river.

FOOLING PREDATORS

Female ducks will risk their own lives in order to protect their ducklings. If a predator approaches, a female duck may pretend to be injured, which makes herself the focus of the predator's attention. She waits for the predator to approach until the last moment, when she suddenly flies out of reach.

As the ducklings grow, they replace their downy feathers with brown feathers similar to female ducks. The young ducks exercise their flight muscles by flapping their wings, but they will be unable to fly until their wing feathers are fully grown.

The ducklings spend more and more time on their own until, eventually, they leave their mother. By the time they are about 8 weeks old the young ducks look like adult females and are able to fly. They are almost fully grown, although they will not have their full adult feathers until they are about 1 year old. The young ducks may stay on the pond where they were born or fly away to find another place to live.

▲ **This young duck is exercising its wings. Soon it will be able to fly.**

▲ This female is nesting in an old tree trunk, which is well hidden from predators.

Habitat

Mallard ducks live in a variety of freshwater habitats, including ponds, lakes, small rivers, marshland and reservoirs. They like areas with open water for feeding, dense vegetation cover for protection, and an open area of land for preening and resting. Occasionally, mallards visit small, sheltered coastal bays and estuaries. Mallards can also be found some distance from water, such as in fields and oak woodland.

UNUSUAL NESTS

Not all mallards nest on the ground. Occasionally they nest in a hollow tree, on a rocky ledge, on a roof or in a window box. From these sites, the newly hatched ducklings must leap from the nest before they are able to fly. Their light, fluffy bodies absorb the bumps and they usually land unhurt.

In the countryside, mallards are often shy and avoid humans. But some become regular visitors to nature reserves, where they get used to human visitors.

In towns and cities, mallards can be found on ponds and boating lakes. These ducks are quite happy to live close to humans, where there are fewer natural predators and more food is available, and they nest and rear their young there. They often become quite tame, getting extra food from people who feed them.

▼ A female mallard with her ducklings sun themselves on the edge of a swimming pool in the city of London.

Migration

After the breeding season, many mallards form
flocks and migrate to warmer areas. When the
breeding season starts again in the spring, they fly
back. Most mallards in Europe are resident, which
means they stay in the same place all year round.
But in the colder northern and eastern parts of
Europe, and in North America, mallards migrate
south in the winter when lakes and ponds turn
to ice.

▲ The patch of dark
blue feathers on the
wings of both male
and female ducks is
a visual signal that
helps a flock keep
together in flight.

▲ When coming down to land, a duck opens its wings to slow it down and extends its legs so it lands feet first.

FLYING

Mallards are very strong fliers and can fly long distances. Migrating mallards can fly at speeds of 60 kilometres an hour, often at great heights. They are able to take off from land or water by launching themselves almost straight into the air. When returning to water, they can fly down at a steep angle, which means they can land on a small area of water, such as a pond.

When they migrate, mallards fly in small groups, often in V-shaped flocks. Each flock usually contains between 10 and 20 mallards, but there can be several hundred. The ducks know when it is time to migrate by sensing the changes in daylight. Before they leave, the ducks become restless and spend more time feeding to build up their reserves of body fat for the journey.

Food

Mallard ducks are omnivores. They eat a wide variety of foods, including plants, seeds and aquatic invertebrates. Mallards are very adaptable and can find food both on land and in the water.

▼ **Mallards are at the centre of several food chains. Cats and rats are mainly a danger just to the eggs and chicks. (The illustrations are not to scale.)**

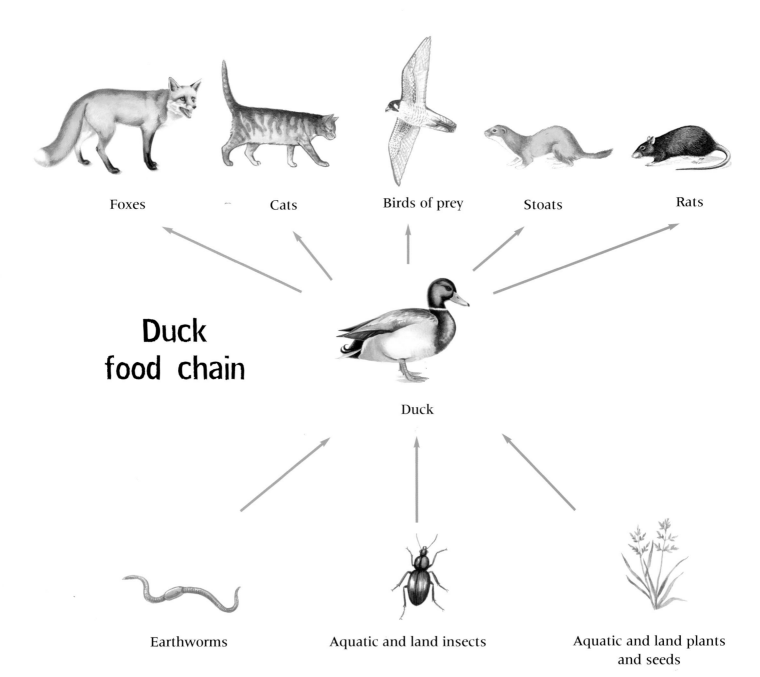

Foxes   Cats   Birds of prey   Stoats   Rats

Duck food chain

Duck

Earthworms   Aquatic and land insects   Aquatic and land plants and seeds

On land, mallards eat plants and seeds, or feed on invertebrates such as insects and earthworms. On water, ducks feed on a variety of plants both above and below the surface. They also eat invertebrates in the water such as insect larvae and freshwater snails.

Mallards sometimes feed on grain in fields of crops, or on acorns in woodland. Domestic ducks are usually given grain to eat but since they are allowed to wander freely, they also forage for food themselves.

CROPS

Mallards are one of the few species of ducks that regularly feed on crops, particularly barley and wheat. In late summer, when the crops are ripe, mallards gather in mixed flocks of young and old ducks. On early mornings and late evenings they can be seen flying to or from the fields to feed.

▼ A female mallard filters out tiny food items with her beak on the shallow edge of a pond.

Feeding

Mallard ducks are also known as puddle, or dabbling, ducks. The name 'puddle' refers to their preference for shallow water or marshy areas. 'Dabbling' describes their main method of feeding, dipping their beak beneath the water.

The mallard's flattened beak has special ridges inside. These catch tiny plants and animals as the duck opens and closes its beak near the surface of the water. The ridges also help to grip and pull up vegetation.

▼ On the side of this female duck's beak, you can clearly see the ridges that help to filter out food.

Although mallards cannot dive for food like some other ducks, they have another way of reaching vegetation on the bottom of a pond. This is called up-ending. The mallard's tail sticks out of the water while its head points down to the bottom, reaching for vegetation beneath. The mallard paddles gently with its feet to help it stay upside down.

▲ A male up-ending to reach food at the bottom of the pond.

Finding a Mate

Male and female mallards are ready to mate when they are a year old. In early spring, a drake will establish a territory. If another drake comes near, he may quack and peck at it to drive it away.

The drake attracts a hen by displaying his courtship feathers, including his bottle-green head and curled tail feathers. On the water the drake performs a special courtship dance. He fluffs up his feathers, waggles his tail and nods his head.

An interested female will respond by swimming behind her new mate, flicking her beak over one side of her body and quacking. The drake responds by turning the back of his head towards the female and swimming slowly away, inviting her to follow.

▼ **This drake is calling out a warning to another drake to get out of his territory.**

MOULTING

Not long after the drake leaves the female, he moults, including all his flight feathers. For the next month, when the drakes are unable to fly away from predators, they grow temporary, dull brown feathers, similar to the female. These dull feathers help to keep the drake hidden from predators until his new flight feathers have grown. Female ducks moult after their young have left.

▲ A female mallard swims closely beside a male to show she has chosen him as her mate.

The drake and hen choose a nest site together, but only the hen builds the nest and stays with her eggs. After about ten days, the drake abandons the hen, although sometimes the same pairs are formed the following year.

Mallards usually only raise one brood a year, but if their eggs or chicks are taken by predators early in the summer, a pair may raise another one or two broods. However, each successive clutch will contain fewer eggs.

Threats

Mallards live to the age of 4 or 5 years in the wild, although domestic ducks may live to the age of 10 or more. Adult mallards have many natural predators, including foxes, cats, stoats and birds of prey. The most dangerous time of year for adult ducks is the four weeks at the end of the breeding season, when they lose their flight feathers and are unable to fly away from predators.

▼ **This European red fox has caught a male mallard, which it will take to a safe place to eat.**

Mallard eggs and chicks are taken by birds that raid nests, such as crows and magpies. They may also be eaten by rats. Ducklings are most at risk in their first ten weeks, before they can fly. On large lakes and rivers, ducklings are also attacked from beneath by pikes, an aggressive predatory fish.

▼ Ducks stand little chance against a falcon's sharp talons. This peregrine falcon has caught a mallard, which it will pluck before eating.

MIGRATION HAZARDS

Migrating mallards face many dangers. If they don't find enough food along the journey, they will become weak and vulnerable to predators. Ducks that stop to eat on fields of grain can be shot by farmers who want to protect their crops. They can also be shot by duck hunters. There are even dangers in mid-flight. In one bizarre incident, a mallard was struck by a commercial airliner while flying at 6.4 kilometres above the Nevada Desert, in the USA.

People and ducks

While mallard ducks benefit from living close to humans, people can also be a major threat. Building developments have destroyed many of the ducks' food and nest sites over the last 50 years by draining their wetland habitats.

The mallard is also a popular game bird and many thousands are shot each year. Sometimes this is done to reduce populations of mallards that may be over-feeding on important habitats or crops. Although many people disagree with duck shooting, either for sport or for pest control, it does not threaten the survival of the species and mallard numbers are not in decline.

▼ Hunters use plastic ducks to attract live ducks so they come close enough to shoot.

▲ **This duckling has drowned after becoming entangled in fishing line left behind by fishermen.**

FEEDING DUCKS

Feeding ducks can be fun and good for the birds as long as it is done properly. The best food to feed ducks is grain, which you can buy from pet shops. Ducks can be fed with brown bread, but only in small amounts. If the ducks stop eating, do not be tempted to throw in more bread. The uneaten food may pollute the water and cause disease.

Ponds and lakes that have become polluted by household, industrial or agricultural waste can poison ducks. Dangerous objects that are dumped in ponds by people can cause injury.

Town and city ponds can become over-populated with ducks, attracted by food fed by people. The water can become polluted from their faeces or, more commonly, from food thrown into the water. Too much uneaten food can attract rats and cause diseases such as food poisoning, which can kill ducks. These diseases can also spread to other waterfowl living on the pond.

27

Duck Life Cycle

1 Mallard eggs hatch four weeks after they are laid. The chicks are born covered with downy feathers and with their eyes closed.

2 Within two hours of hatching, the ducklings' eyes are open and they can run around.

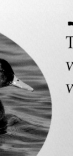

5 The next spring, when they are 1 year old, male and female ducks are able to mate.

4 Ducklings first fly when they are about 8 weeks old.

3 When they are only a day or two old, the ducklings swim for the first time.

Duck Clues

Look out for the following clues to help you find signs of a duck:

Nest
The shallow nest is lined with grasses on the ground near a pond. Look out for a female mallard on her nest, especially in towns and cities where the nests are often less hidden. Never approach a duck's nest because the mother may abandon her eggs and they will not hatch.

Nest building
You may see a female mallard uprooting vegetation and carrying it in her beak. She is collecting materials to build her nest.

Winter gathering
A good time to see mallards is in the winter, when large numbers gather together for safety on water. Some may be migrants from another country.

Courtship display
Spring courtship displays, which include head nodding, can be seen on freshwater in the countryside or in towns and cities.

Ducklings
Spring is a good time to see a mother and her ducklings on the water.

Call
Female ducks makes a loud 'quack' sound, while males call a low-pitched 'rhab-rhab'.

Eggshells
Grey-green or yellowish-brown eggshells can be found after the eggs have hatched.

Footprints
The webbed footprints of mallards may be seen on the muddy edges of ponds and lakes. They show the three toes pointing forwards and one toe pointing backwards.

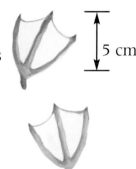

5 cm

Droppings
Mallard droppings are green and semi-liquid when fresh. Sometimes they contain undigested plant matter, depending on what has been eaten.

Feathers
Look for mallard feathers around ponds and streams after they have moulted in late summer. Brown feathers are from a female, while green or grey feathers are from a male.

Silhouette
Mallard ducks, geese and swans are often seen in flight, near water or when flying from one place to another. The mallard has broader wings and a shorter tail than most ducks.

Glossary

aquatic Lives in water.

brood A group of chicks born at the same time.

buoyant Able to float on water.

camouflage The colour or pattern of some animals that helps them blend in with their surroundings and makes them hard to see.

clutch A number of eggs laid at the same time by one female.

courtship The behaviour of animals before they mate.

domestic An animal that is bred as a pet or to supply food.

down Soft feathers that help keep a chick or adult bird warm.

drake A male duck.

duckling A young duck.

embryo The stage of life inside an egg.

estuary An area around a river mouth, where a river meets the sea.

forage To search for food.

freshwater Water in ponds, rivers and lakes that does not contain seawater.

habitat The natural home of an animal or plant.

hen A female duck or other bird.

incubate To sit on eggs to keep them warm until they hatch.

invertebrates Small animals that do not have a backbone. Worms, spiders and insects are invertebrates.

migration Travelling between different habitats or countries in particular seasons.

moult To shed fur or feathers so they can be replaced by new ones.

omnivore An animal that eats all types of food, both animal and plants.

predator An animal that eats other animals.

preen To keep feathers in good condition by arranging and cleaning them with the beak.

prey Animals that are killed and eaten by predators.

resident An animal that lives in a country and does not migrate.

territory The area that is defended and controlled by an animal.

up-ending Feeding method, when the duck's tail end is above water while the head reaches down below.

wetlands Habitats that contain water such as lakes or ponds.

wingspan The distance from one wing tip to the other of a bird with its wings spread out.

Finding Out More

Other books to read

Animal Classification by Polly Goodman (Hodder Wayland, 2004)

Animal Young: Birds by Rod Theodorou (Heinemann, 1999)

Classifying Living Things: Classifying Birds by Andrew Solway (Heinemann, 2003)

From Egg to Adult: The Life Cycle of Birds by Mike Unwin (Heinemann, 2003)

Illustrated Encyclopedia of Animals by Fran Pickering (Chrysalis, 2003)

Junior Nature Guides: Birds (Chrysalis, 2001)

Life Cycles: Ducks and Other Birds by Sally Morgan (Chrysalis, 2001)

Living Nature: Birds by Angela Royston (Chrysalis, 2002)

The Wayland Book of Common British Birds by Nick Williams (Hodder Wayland, 2000)

What's the Difference?: Birds by Stephen Savage (Hodder Wayland, 2002)

Wild Britain: Towns & Cities, Parks & Gardens by R. & L. Spilsbury (Heinemann, 2003)

Wild Habitats of the British Isles: Rivers & Waterways; Towns & Cities by R. & L. Spilsbury (Heinemann, 2005)

Organisations to contact

Countryside Foundation for Education
PO Box 8, Hebden Bridge HX7 5YJ
www.countrysidefoundation.org.uk
An organisation that produces training and teaching materials to help the understanding of the countryside and its problems.

English Nature
Northminster House, Peterborough, Cambridgeshire PE1 1UA
www.englishnature.org.uk
A government body that promotes the conservation of English wildlife and the natural environment.

RSPB
The Lodge, Sandy, Bedfordshire SG19 2DL
www.rspb.org.uk
A wild birds conservation charity with wildlife reserves and a website that includes an A-Z of UK birds, news, surveys and webcams about issues concerning wild birds.

Wildlife Watch
National Office, The Kiln, Waterside, Mather Road, Newark NG24 1WT
www.wildlifetrusts.org
The junior branch of the Wildlife Trusts, a network of local Wildlife Trusts caring for nearly 2,500 nature reserves, from rugged coastline to urban wildlife havens, protecting a huge number of habitats and species.

Index

Page numbers in **bold** refer to a photograph or illustration.